Druid presents

THE NEW ELECTRIC BALLROOM

by Enda Walsh

BREDA	**Rosaleen Linehan**
CLARA	**Val Lilley**
ADA	**Catherine Walsh**
PATSY	**Mikel Murfi**

DIRECTOR	**Enda Walsh**
DESIGNER	**Sabine Dargent**
LIGHTING DESIGNER	**Sinéad McKenna**
SOUND DESIGNER	**Gregory Clarke**
CASTING DIRECTOR	**Maureen Hughes**

Production Manager	Eamonn Fox
Company Stage Manager	Sarah Lynch
Stage Director	Lee Davis
Assistant Stage Manager (Galway)	Colm O'Callaghan
(Edinburgh)	Jen Raith
Technical Manager	Barry O'Brien
Costume Supervisor	Doreen McKenna
Wigs and Make-up	Val Sherlock
Carpenters	Gus Dewar
	Tony Cording
Publicist	Kate Bowe PR

Graphic Design	Bite! Associates
Cover Image Photographer	Ros Kavanagh
Production Photographer	Keith Pattison

**14 – 26 JULY 2008 DRUID THEATRE, GALWAY
as part of Galway Arts Festival**

**3 – 24 AUGUST 2008 TRAVERSE THEATRE, EDINBURGH
as part of the Edinburgh Festival Fringe 2008**

The New Electric Ballroom received its premiere at the Kammerspiel Theatre, Munich, on 30 September 2004.

DRUID

'Druid continues to set the Irish standard' The Guardian

'A highlight not just of my theatregoing year but of my theatregoing life'
The New York Times on DruidSynge

Druid was founded in Galway in 1975 by graduates of NUI Galway, Mick Lally, Marie Mullen and Garry Hynes – the first professional theatre company in Ireland to be based outside Dublin. Since then Druid has toured extensively in Ireland and recent international touring includes visits to London, Edinburgh, Sydney, Perth, Washington, D.C., New York and Tokyo. The company has had two artistic directors: Garry Hynes (1975–91 and 1995 to date) and Maeliosa Stafford (1991–94).

Druid brings groundbreaking work from its base in Chapel Lane to audiences in Galway, throughout Ireland and around the world. In 1996 Druid premiered Martin McDonagh's debut work *The Beauty Queen of Leenane*, in a co-production with the Royal Court Theatre. It opened in Galway and subsequently played in London, Sydney, Dublin, and on Broadway, where the production won four Tony Awards. In 1997 it formed part of The Leenane Trilogy. More recent productions include *Long Day's Journey into Night* (2007).

DruidSynge, the company's critically acclaimed production of all six of John Millington Synge's plays on the same day, premiered at the Galway Arts Festival in 2005 and has since toured to Dublin, Edinburgh, Inis Meáin, Minneapolis and New York.

The Walworth Farce, written by Enda Walsh, was commissioned by Druid and received its premiere at the Town Hall Theatre, Galway in 2006. Since then, it has gone on to win a Fringe First at the 2007 Edinburgh Festival Fringe and achieved further acclaim from the New York critics during its 2008 run at St Ann's Warehouse, New York.

Through its new-writing programme, Druid has premiered *Leaves* by Lucy Caldwell (2007), *Empress of India* by Stuart Carolan (2006) and *The Walworth Farce* by Enda Walsh (2006).

STAY IN TOUCH
For up-to-date news on Druid, visit our website www.druid.ie and join our mailing list.

SUPPORTING DRUID
For information on how you can support Druid or become a Friend of Druid, please contact us at info@druid.ie or on +353 91 568 660.

Acknowledgements
Druid is grant aided by the Arts Council of Ireland and gratefully
acknowledges the support of Culture Ireland.

Druid wishes to express its continuing gratitude to Thomas McDonagh
& Company Ltd for their support of the company and gratefully acknowledges
the assistance of Galway City Council and Galway County Council.

CAST

ROSALEEN LINEHAN *Breda*

Druid: *The New Electric Ballroom* marks Rosaleen's debut with Druid.

Other theatre: *Juno* (New York City Center); *The House of Bernarda Alba, The Importance of Being Earnest, Mary Makebelieve, Carthaginians* (Abbey Theatre); *Dancing at Lughnasa* (Abbey Theatre, Garrick Theatre, London; Plymouth Theatre, New York); *Mother of all the Behans* (Abbey Theatre, Brighton, Edinburgh, Montreal, New York); *Gates of Gold, Long Day's Journey into Night, Twelfth Night, The Rivals* (Gate Theatre, Dublin); *Happy Days* (Gate Theatre, Dublin; Lincoln Center, New York; Almeida Theatre; Barbican); *Blood Wedding* (Almeida Theatre); *Bailegangaire* (Royal Court Theatre); *Lost in Yonkers, The Plough and the Stars, Blithe Spirit* (Guthrie Theatre, Minneapolis); *The Dead* (Pittsburgh and Irish Classical Theatre); *Tartuffe* (Roundabout Theatre, New York); *The Cripple of Inishmaan* (Geffen Playhouse, Los Angeles); *On the Loose, Des and Rosie Ride Again* (Irish tour).

Film & Television: *Bittersweet; Happy Days; Conamara* (Boje Buck Films); *About Adam* (Venus Productions); *Mad About Mambo; The Hi-Lo Country, The Butcher Boy.*

VAL LILLEY *Clara*

Druid: *On Raftery's Hill.*

Other theatre: *Loyal Women, Flying Blind, Inventing a Colour* (Royal Court Theatre); *Blue Heart* (Royal Court/Out of Joint & tour); *Holy Mothers* (Ambassadors Theatre); *The Mai, A Love Song for Ulster, Once a Catholic, Factory Girls* (Tricycle Theatre); *Killing the Cat* (for Soho Poly, Royal Court Theatre); *The True Life of Fiction of Mata Hari* (Palace Theatre, Watford); *Fen, Far Away, Jane Eyre* (Crucible Theatre, Sheffield); *The Beauty Queen of Leenane* (Salisbury Playhouse); *Drive On* (Lyric Theatre, Belfast); *Pig's Ear, Breezeblock Park, Shadow of a Gunman, Who's Afraid of Virginia Woolf?* (Liverpool Playhouse); *Lysistrata* (Contact Theatre, Manchester); *Blood Wedding, My Mother Said I Never Should* (Octagon Theatre, Bolton); *The Cherry Orchard, The Card* (New Victoria Theatre, Stoke); *Madness in Goa* (Oldham Coliseum); *Who's Afraid of Virginia Woolf?* (Nottingham Playhouse & Everyman Theatre).

Film & Television: *The Commander* (La Plante Productions); *Serious and Organised, Court Drama, Messiah 3, Courtroom* (Mersey TV); *The Catherine Tate Show, Grange Hill, Crime and Punishment, Hope and Glory, EastEnders, Children of the North* (BBC); *Anybody's Nightmare* (Carlton); *Elidor, Missing Persons, The Famous Five* (ITV); *The Rag Nymph, First Communion Day, Peak Practice, Scully, The Refuge, Final Run, Nice Town, Albion Market, Coronation Street, The Riff Raff Element* (Granada); *Blood on the Dole* (Channel 4).

CATHERINE WALSH *Ada*

Druid: *DruidSynge* (Galway, Dublin, Edinburgh, Inis Meáin, Minneapolis and New York); *Empress of India* (Galway and Dublin Theatre Festival 2006); *The Year of the Hiker* (Galway, Dublin and national tour), *Sharon's Grave, Werewolves.*

Other theatre: *Fool for Love, Eden, The Gigli Concert, Translations, Kevin's Bed, Blackwater Angel, At Swim Two Birds, Love in the Title* (Abbey and Peacock Theatres); *Dancing at Lughnasa, A Christmas Carol, Phaedra* (Gate Theatre, Dublin); *Buddleia, From Both Hips, Licking the Marmalade Spoon, The Chastitute, Big Maggie.*

Film & Television: *The Family, The Ambassador, Holby City* (BBC); *On Home Ground* (RTÉ); *The Last September, Whatever Happened to Bridget Cleary* (RTÉ, Wildfire Films).

Radio: *All That Fall, Eden, The Monotonous Life of Little Miss P, Swanscross, Shiftwork.*

MIKEL MURFI *Patsy*

Mikel trained at École Jacques Lecoq, Paris.

Druid: As an actor, *The Increased Difficulty of Concentration*. As a director, *The Walworth Farce*.

Other theatre: As an actor, *The Chairs* (Blue Raincoat, Sligo); *The Cure* (Half Moon Theatre, Cork); *The Clerk and the Clown, Playing A Round* (Galway Arts Festival); *The Morning After Optimism, The Playboy of the Western World* (Peacock Theatre); *The Tempest, The Comedy of Errors* (Abbey Theatre); *Stokehauling, SickDyingDeadBuriedOut, Half Eight Mass of a Tuesday, Come Down from The Mountain John Clown, John Clown, Macbeth* (Barabbas); *God's Gift* (Barabbas national tour); *The White Headed Boy* (Barabbas, national and US tours); *Studs, Melting Penguins* (Passion Machine); *Lady Windermere's Fan* (Rough Magic). *The Tender Trap* (Pigsback). As a director, *Diamonds in The Soil, The Lost Days of Ollie Deasy* (Macnas); *The Mysteries* (co-director, Macnas); *Trad* (Galway Arts Festival Production); *The Lonesome West* (Lyric Theatre, Belfast).

Film & Television: As an actor, *Ella Enchanted, The Last September, Sweety Barrett, The Butcher Boy, Love and Rage, Guiltrip, Words Upon the Window Pane, The Three Joes, The Commitments*. As a director, *Druma* (a short film for Macnas); *John Duffy's Brother* (Parkfilms).

CREATIVE TEAM

ENDA WALSH Writer and Director

Druid: *The New Electric Ballroom* is Enda's second play with Druid; *The Walworth Farce.*

Other theatre: *The Walworth Farce* (Galway, Cork, Dublin, Edinburgh 2007, Fringe First Winner, New York); *Chatroom* (Cottesloe, Royal National Theatre, March 2006, Autumn 2007); *The Small Things* (Paines Plough at the Menier Chocolate Factory, London and Galway Arts Festival 2005); *The New Electric Ballroom* (Kammerspeil Theatre Munich, winner of Theater Heute's Best Foreign Play 2005); two short plays, *How These Men Talk* (Zurich Shauspielehaus) and *Lynndie's Gotta Gun* (for Artistas Unidos at Lisbon's National Theatre); *bedbound* (Dublin Theatre Festival 2000, Edinburgh 2001, Fringe First Winner, Royal Court, London, New York and worldwide); *misterman* (Granary Theatre); *Disco Pigs* (Cork, Dublin, 1996, Edinburgh 1997, West End 1998; awarded Arts Council Playwrights Award 1996, Best Fringe Production 1996, Stewart Parker and George Devine Awards 1997); *The Ginger Ale Boy* (Corcadorca).

Forthcoming this Autumn: *Delirium*, an adaptation of Dostoevsky's *The Brothers Karamazov* for Theatre O (Abbey Theatre and Barbican).

Film: *Disco Pigs* (Temple Films/Renaissance); *Hunger* (Blast/FILMFOUR – winner of the Camera D'Or and international prize in Cannes 2008. Released in October).

In development: *Chatroom* (for Ruby Films/FILMFOUR and Scott Rudin Films); *Island of the Aunts* (Cuba Pictures), an adaptation of Eva Ibbotson's children's novel; *Kinderboy* (BBC).

Radio: *Four Big Days in the Life of Dessie Banks* (RTÉ Radio; winner of the PPI Award for Best Radio Drama 2001); *The Monotonous Life of Little Miss P* (BBC; commended in the Berlin Prix Europa 2003).

SABINE DARGENT Set and Costume Designer

Druid: *The Walworth Farce* (nominated for an Irish Times Theatre Award 2006).

Other theatre: *City Fusion* (St Patrick's Parade); *The Pride of Parnell Street* (Dublin, London, New Haven); *Circus* (Dublin); *The Lonesome West* (Ireland); *The Bacchae of Baghdad, The Importance of Being Earnest* (Abbey Theatre); *Antigone, Hard to Believe* (Storytellers); *Henry and Harriet* (Belfast); *To Have and To Hold* (Old Museum, Belfast); *Days of Wine and Roses* (Lyric); *Dublin Carol* (Everyman Palace, Cork); *Ghosts* (winner ESB/Irish Times Best Set Design Award, 2003), *Monged, Pilgrims in the Park, Tadhg Stray Wandered In* (Fishamble); *How Many Miles to Babylon?* (Second Age); *The Shadow of the Glen, The Tinker's Wedding* (Big Telly); *Martha, Little Rudolf* (Barnstorm); *Jack Fell Down, Burning Dreams, Last Call* (Team); *The Tempest* (Blue Raincoat); *Desert Lullaby* (Gallowglass); *Hysteria* (b*spoke). Sabine has also worked with Theatre A Grande Vitesse (Paris), Théâtre de Châtillon and L'Epée de Bois in France.

SINÉAD MCKENNA Lighting Designer

Druid: *The New Electric Ballroom* is Sinéad's first design with Druid.

Other theatre: *The Parker Project, Life is a Dream, Attempts on Her Life, Dream of Autumn, Improbable Frequency* (Rough Magic); *The Burial at Thebes, Howie the Rookie, Finders Keepers* (Peacock Theatre); *Last Days of the Celtic Tiger, Blackbird* (Landmark); *Circus* (Barabbas); *Private Lives* (Gate Theatre); *Honour* (b*spoke); *Macbeth, Philadelphia Here I Come, Othello, How Many Miles to Babylon?* (Second Age); *All Over Town, Wunderkind* (Calipo); *Henceforward* (Derby Playhouse); *God's Grace, Adrenalin, Ladies and Gents* (Irish Times Theatre Award for Best Lighting Design) (Semper Fi); *Scenes from a Watercooler, The Real Thing, Dinner with Friends* (Gúna Nua); *Candide, The Butterfly Ranch* (Performance Corporation); *Shooting Gallery* (Bedrock); *The Snow Queen, Merry Christmas Betty Ford* (Lyric Theatre); *The Gist of It* (Fishamble); *Hard to Believe* (Storytellers); *The Woman Who Walked into Doors* (Upbeat Productions); *Diarmaid and Grainne* (Passion Machine).

Dance and Opera: *Does She Take Sugar?* (for Jean Butler); *Swept* (CoisCéim); *As a Matter of Fact* (Dance Theatre of Ireland); *La Bohème* (Co-Opera).

Sinéad has also designed *Bovinity* for Tommy Tiernan; *Tongues* for Des Bishop; *Fitting In* for Neil Delamere; and Maeve Higgins' *Ha Ha Yum*.

GREGORY CLARKE Sound Designer

Druid: *The Hackney Office.*

Other theatre: *The Vortex* (Apollo Theatre); *Ring Round the Moon* (Playhouse Theatre); *Cloud Nine* (Almeida Theatre); *Pygmalion* (American Airlines, Broadway); *Equus, And Then There Were None, Some Girls* (Gielgud Theatre); *Journey's End* (London, UK tour and Broadway; New York Drama Desk Award winner for Outstanding Sound Design); *A Voyage Round My Father, Honour* (Wyndhams Theatre); *The Philanthropist* (Donmar Warehouse); *Hayfever, Lady Windermere's Fan, The Royal Family* (Theatre Royal, Haymarket); *The Home Place, Whose Life is it Anyway?* (Comedy Theatre); *The Emperor Jones, The Chairs* (Gate Theatre, London); *Waiting for Godot, Abigail's Party* (New Ambassadors Theatre); *What the Butler Saw* (Criterion Theatre); *The Dresser* (Duke of York's Theatre); *Amy's View, You Never Can Tell* (Garrick Theatre); *National Anthems* (Old Vic); *Betrayal* (Duchess Theatre); *Mum's the Word* (Albery Theatre); *Song of Singapore* (Mayfair Theatre); *No Man's Land, Tristan and Yseult, The Emperor Jones* (National Theatre); *Great Expectations, Coriolanus, The Merry Wives of Windsor, Tantalus, Cymbeline* (RSC); *Troilus and Cressida* (European tour); *The English Game* (UK tour); *Blackbird* (UK tour); *Crown Matrimonial* (UK tour); *Uncle Vanya* (The Rose, Kingston); *Pygmalion, Little Nell, Measure For Measure, Habeas Corpus, Miss Julie, Private Lives, Much Ado About Nothing, You Can Never Tell, Design for Living, Betrayal, Fight for Barbara, As You Like It* (The Peter Hall Company); *The Changeling* (Barbican); *Nights at the Circus* (Lyric Hammersmith and tour); *Insignificance* (Sheffield Lyceum); *My Boy Jack* (UK tour).

THE NEW ELECTRIC BALLROOM

Enda Walsh

To Jo Ellison

Characters

BREDA, *sixties*

CLARA, *sixties*

ADA, *forty*

PATSY, *a fishmonger*

This text went to press before the end of rehearsals and so may differ slightly from the play as performed.

A living room/kitchen space.

On a wall, three different sets of clothes hanging on separate hangers. A cashmere jumper and a rara skirt; a 1950's red blouse and a blue pleated skirt; and a glitzy show-business man's suit.

A small kitchen counter with a large delicious-looking sponge cake on it.

The atmosphere immediately taut and aggressive.

Two older women, in their sixties, BREDA *and* CLARA, *and a younger one,* ADA, *who is forty.*

CLARA *is sitting.* BREDA *is standing in the corner facing the wall.* ADA *is standing right behind her, staring intently at the back of her head.* ADA *slightly out of breath. She's holding some lipstick in her hand.*

BREDA (*fast and frightened*). By their nature people are talkers. You can't deny that. You could but you'd be affirming what you're trying to argue against and what would the point of that be? No point. Just adding to the sea of words that already exist out there in your effort to say that people are not talkers. But people talk and no one in their right mind would challenge that. Unless you're one of those poor souls starved of vocal cords or that Willy Prendergast boy who used live in town and only managed three words. One was 'yes', one was 'no' and one was 'fish'. Yes yes yes. No no no. Fish fish fish. Fish yes yes. Fish no no. Yes no fish. No yes fish. Fish no fish. Fish yes fish. So even he talked.

CLARA. Look at my little feet.

BREDA. People are born talkers. Those present when a baby comes into the world are made all too aware that the womb is a more desirable place for a baby. That and the unglamorous entrance the baby must make. For all his miracles and great creations, you'd imagine our Lord could have created a more dignified point of arrival. This is the man who did wonders with the mouth and ears and surpassed Himself with the eyes but sharing a channel with the 'waterworks department' doesn't strike me as the healthiest environment for a yet-to-be-born baby and I'm not even a plumber.

CLARA. Would you look at these tiny little hands!

BREDA. People talking just for the act of it. Words spinning to nothing. For no definable reason. Like a little puppy, a hungry puppy yapping for his supper, yap-yap-yap-yap… that's people with words. The breath and the word are interchangeable. Interchangeable!? Identical. Of course people breathe to live. While they talk to…

CLARA. I'm getting smaller! I worry too much. Worry does that, Ada. It does! It stunts you, does worry! Look at the size of me in this chair. Like a midget!

ADA. You're not a midget.

CLARA. A cup of tea, a cup of tea will sort me out.

BREDA. Won't make you any taller.

CLARA (*snaps*). There's nothing I can't see from here, bitch!

ADA. How could you know that?

CLARA. Instinct.

ADA. Christ…

CLARA. Aren't we ever going to have tea again? Where's my tea?

ADA (*mimicking*). 'Where's my tea? Where's my tea?'

CLARA. Fetch me my tea, 'Breda the bad girl'.

ADA. There'll be no tea today. (*Turns back and snaps.*) Breda!

BREDA. For that's people with their great need to talk. The terrible necessity of it. And even besides the talking, far deeper than the talking, is this need to connect somehow. To belong. We're out into the world and all is noise and light and we're speaking of the womb being a more desirable place and it's like the nurse has given us a pill.

CLARA (*mumbles longingly*). Oh, what chance a pill?

BREDA. And the pill gives us this need to belong to 'mother', to 'father', to 'brothers and sisters' and 'in-laws' and 'friends' and 'strangers about to be friends' and 'strangers who'll always be strangers'. The talking is important but superficial really, 'cause the pill gives us a greater compulsion to connect with all these people. To be a part.

CLARA. Fish fish fish! Fish yes fish. No yes fish!

BREDA. But here's the thing…

ADA. Turn around now.

BREDA *stops and turns around from the corner and faces* ADA. *Her face is aggressively marked with red lipstick, we guess that it's been done by* ADA. BREDA *holds a ceramic kitchen bowl. Seeing her,* CLARA, *frightened, covers her eyes.*

(*Quietly prompting.*) Wherever…

A slight pause.

BREDA. Wherever that pill resides in the body it doesn't reach the further recesses of the brain. 'Cause sitting back there… back there and likely only to make the odd appearance, is the 'hard truth'…

ADA. Slow.

A pause.

BREDA (*slower*). And the 'hard truth' reminds us that we'll always be alone, baby sister. Besides the yap-yap and the arms outstretched and our great compulsion to be with others, we'll always be back in the womb. Back there and reminding ourselves that the womb is a more desirable place than this 'created world'. We don't want to be alone but we're alone. We don't want to be an island but we are that island.

A pause.

Will I put the piece of paper back in its bowl, Ada?

She does so and ADA *takes the bowl off her.*

ADA (*to* BREDA). Is it true we're alone?

BREDA *nods.*

Us more than anyone else?

BREDA. The same.

BREDA *touches her nose. Blood spills down her face.* ADA *just looks at her.*

CLARA (*announcing*). Nobody… Makes… Cake… Like… You… Clara.

BREDA *goes to sit down.*

Our mother would always say that. She said I was a born baker. She said I had a gift for coffee cake the way Jesus had a gift for sacrifice. When I was six she'd place me on her lap and I'd mix the flour with the eggs and the sugar and the coffee. And we'd be half-listening to the radio and her leg would send me up and down like I'm on a horse trotting. Not galloping now! Never a gallop. She'd get me to recite the alphabet while the cake stretched out in the heat inside. The lovely pattern of the ABCs over and over as it pumps the air into the sponge. Me and the oven in happy unison, in lovely poetry. Sure, look at the consistency of that sponge cake!

BREDA. Enough, Clara!

BREDA *stares over at* ADA *who is lost in her thoughts.* BREDA *starts removing the lipstick from her face with some baby wipes.*

CLARA. If it was entered into a contest... imagine the envy. Imagine all those old bitches hiding their hate because of my prize. A local photographer is there and their faces looking up at me, Ada. The girls from the cannery looking at me! At me! And I turn to Holy Mary, 'cause she's standing there right beside, and the mother of Jesus takes me aside and says, 'You're the best, Clara. Better than all them who locked you inside. Who spun out the gossip in the cannery and locked that door behind you. You're better than all those bitches.'

BREDA. Clara!

CLARA. So I slice off a piece of cake for the mother of Jesus... and she scoffs it down, not in the least bit like a virgin, but what do you expect, what with the great divinity of this sponge? What colour rosette would they give me for winning with such a great coffee cake? There's too many colours to choose from. What heavenly colour, Ada?

A very long pause.

There's a terrible lull in the conversation. The sort of lull that can get you worrying about other things.

A pause.

Will I take the piece of paper from the bowl, Ada?

ADA *doesn't answer.*

Can we not have a cup of tea and some of that lovely coffee cake I made?

A pause.

BREDA (*to* ADA). Did something happen outside, pet?

A long pause.

ADA. The town still asleep I cycle to work as always. Through the little narrow streets and over the cobble-stones away from the sea and towards the cannery up on the hill. I see a furniture van outside Mrs Cullen's house.

She's getting a new kitchen put in and her stood watching the men carrying the fancy cabinets through her garden and into her house. Her little dog Bobby's bouncing up and down and yapping the way little dogs do. I can see her looking at me as I pass by and a coldness in her face because of what us three are to them. I cycle on and into the cannery and walk through the floor with the loud machines tinning the fish… still echoing with the gossip of Clara and Breda and the Roller Royle. Into my little office and head down and lost in the numbers and turning fish into money. Just me and the machines. No one but me and the sea being tinned. (*Slight pause*.) It's evening and I cycle home and the streets are again empty and that furniture van passes and gets me thinking of Mrs Cullen's new fitted kitchen and for some reason I stop my bike outside her house. And I'm standing there imagining her in a yellow light surrounded by all her new things. (*Pause*.) He's lying on the ground dying. His insides are more out than in. His blond hair stuck with blood and bits. I can see the whole scene played out. The kitchen fitted and Mrs Cullen inside and Bobby bouncing up and down and yapping at the men as they get into the van. And the van pulls away and Bobby closer and closer still and caught under the wheel and laid into the road. I'm seeing all of this played out with Mrs Cullen at her door and walking towards me and then seeing Bobby lying on the road and then bent over getting sick into her begonias… and she's crying now… she's crying. (*Pause*.) I'm standing with my bicycle watching and…!! I start to smile. I'm smiling at a woman and her dying dog. (*Slight pause*.) How is it I've come to feel this way?

A door opens. It's PATSY *the fishmonger with a plastic tray full of large fish.*

PATSY. All right, the ladies?

BREDA. Leave them where you stand and go.

PATSY *puts down the tray.*

PATSY. Terrific news about Nana Cotter, isn't it? A hundred years, God bless her, and a lovely letter from the President of congratulations.

A pause as the sisters don't answer.

To mark the occasion she got her hair done in a purple rinse and a party was thrown with all manner of vol-au-vents and trifle present.

A pause as the sisters remain silent.

Poor love got a little excited and shit herself…

CLARA. Would you look at these tiny little feet!

PATSY. Yeah, she's a great woman, Nana, all right. Little bones like summer kindling, hands like pigeon's feet, hearing shot from years of working in the cannery but by Jesus can she eat trifle? Eat it? Like a Hoover!

A pause. He doesn't want to leave, despite it being obvious he's an unwelcome guest.

Mr Simmons got his hip done. Looks a hell of lot more normal than before. Great to see him back all level. He's a sprightly ninety-year-old, despite all his misfortunes. Feck it, he's had that many trips to the garage, he's more plastic than flesh, but to see his little cataract eyes lit up with renewed life…

BREDA. You can go now, we're busy.

PATSY. But what a lovely smell of coffee cake in here. Different houses have their own stamp. I could close my eyes and still make my way around town if the front doors were open. I'd be the first to say I'm not the sharpest knife in the rack and I'm no looker either. People have said I have the looks of a man who's been struck in the face by a wet fish and I couldn't argue with that for the truth is I have often been struck by a wet fish in the face. Several times in fact. But when it comes to smelling things… well, boys!! You won't find a keener nose in the whole of the county! Obviously some people think that's an unfortunate ability, what with me being a fishmonger, and they wouldn't be wrong...

CLARA (*blocks her ears and mumbles*). Yes no no! No yes fish! Fish fish fish...

PATSY. But God, that was a great night the other night! Mags Donald had all her grandchildren in the pub and while I was only passing through to use the gents I had to stop a while and listen to the great sing-along. Like a lark her little crippled grandson sang and we were all reduced to tears when Mags got up and said what a gift from God this little spastic was. But feck it, what breeding! Like their own village they were. Masses of them spread around her feet like Mags herself was giving a sermon at the Mount and though no loaves and fishes were present there was plenty of crisps and scampi...

BREDA (*snaps*). What is it, Patsy!?

A pause. Again he looks towards the open door and then back.

PATSY. Things are odd. (*Slight pause.*) Outside.

BREDA. Tell him stop, Ada!

ADA *lowers her head.*

Leave!

PATSY. I'm standing in the little shoebox I call my bedroom, Ada. I'm standing in my underpants. I'm standing there staring down on my little bed, the sheets all creased and...? Like skin. The pillow dented from where I lay my head. The shape of me marked out on the bed, mapping out my night's sleep. And for some reason that gets me nervous so that I have to leave the room. The house quiet as always. The little stairs groaning as always. Everything as always but for this ball of butterflies growing inside me. So I dress real quick and leave and off and out to work. I'm outside then. And the narrow cobbled streets of the town are a bit uneasy underfoot. The narrow streets narrower somehow.

The houses on either side, they're leaning in that bit close to me. They're squeezing me, hurrying me towards work. I come to the little harbour to gather up my fish from the boats like I always do. I say hello to Simple Paddy who helps out in the harbour tying up the boats. I listen to his dream from the night before, the way I always do listen. It takes some listening because of his cleft palate but I listen all the same. Anyway I'm being smacked with that much spit that I have to look away. And I see over his shoulder that the seas are getting smaller. They're getting smaller. I look up to the cliffs and it really looks like the cliffs are receding. Can sort of feel the seas and cliffs being drawn back in and disappearing and becoming butterflies inside me. I have that feeling that today will be the start of my last day. (*He covers his eyes.*) I can see a picture of me running from your house. My heart's been ripped out and the ground underneath is loose underfoot. I'm running towards the harbour from this cliff. I can see the harbour being sucked into the sand and the cliffs pulled back like you would pull a curtain back. There's a great space now with me running over it towards nothing, towards…! No place. My heart's been ripped out, yet I can't stop running.

A pause. He lowers his hands from his eyes.

I can see all this… and then I'm back on the harbour with Simple Paddy and his cleft palate spitting over me.

A pause.

ADA. From this house you ran?

PATSY. Yes, Ada, from here.

BREDA. Leave, Patsy!

PATSY *leaves with* BREDA *slamming the door closed behind him.*

Why is it you allowed him to talk like that!?

ADA *marches over to a small table where an old tape recorder stands.*

ADA (*snaps*). Quiet!

> ADA *rewinds a tape*.

CLARA. It's time, then.

> CLARA *stands and she and* BREDA *watch* ADA'*s every move*.

Won't you say who it is, Ada, please? Is it Breda the bad girl?

> *The tape stops.* ADA *presses the play button and what begins is a foley soundtrack roughly pasted together by* ADA *to accompany the story we're about to hear.*

ADA. It's time and looking in the mirror and this feeling of everything not too right...

CLARA. Whose story, Ada?

ADA. It's time and looking in the mirror and this feeling...

CLARA. Ada?

ADA. ...of everything not too right, not too right. Up in the bathroom and my eighteen-year-old body...

CLARA. ...tries to shake off these...

ADA. Louder!

CLARA. ...tries to shake off these...

ADA. Louder, Clara!

CLARA. ...tries to shake off these doubts. Staring back behind the blusher and eyeshadow a girl who's yet to be kissed. Properly kissed.

ADA. Been mauled in the car park...

CLARA. Been mauled in the car park once outside The Sunshine Ballroom. Mauled by Jimbo 'The Face' Byrne, a fisherman stinking of stout and mackerel with the biggest face in the west. Crushed me up against his Ford Cortina and tore at my tits. Jimbo's head like an old horse all stooped and drunk. His fish fingers like hooks on my good blouse. But never been properly kissed...

ADA. But thoughts of him…

CLARA. Yes, thoughts of 'him' have me more forward thinking.

BREDA starts to undress CLARA down to her slip.

ADA. Louder.

CLARA. Thoughts of 'him' have me more forward thinking. For weren't they his words that asked me to meet him backstage? Wasn't it him that placed us together with that promise…

ADA. You meet me after.

CLARA. 'You meet me after.' And butterflies carry me down stairs. The soles of my feet tingling 'cause of 'him'. The top of my head all fizz! It's my time. It's my time.

ADA. You smell nice.

CLARA. Dad's voice stuck behind the newspaper and I tuck into my Saturday fry.

The rustling newspaper has me in mind of the crowd that'll gather tonight.

ADA. You meet me after.

CLARA. Packed so tight and faced towards the stage, we are. Clothes sparking off each other, shined leather shoes sticking on the dance floor. The chatter loud so you can't hear words and only these crackling noises. I polish off the bacon in double-quick time!

ADA and BREDA grunt like pigs.

ADA. Do it!

CLARA grunts like a pig, joining ADA and BREDA in the grunting.

BREDA nonchalantly walks to the wall and takes down the 1950's rara skirt and the cashmere jumper.

ADA stops grunting.

Sweet Breda.

CLARA. And through the door and Breda too made-up for the dance. Made-up in her nice blue skirt and red blouse… (*Suddenly forgets*.)

ADA. Her silent as usual! Mother slides…

CLARA. What?

ADA. Her silent as usual!

CLARA. Her silent as usual. Mother slides her fry towards her and like a little bird, her bites of the bacon. Like a little birdy! The rustling of the newspaper and her little lady bites. Her little lady bites. Her little lady bites! (*Mimics the birdlike noises and bites of* BREDA. *Snaps*.) 'Can't you eat like a humanfuckingbeing?!'

BREDA *starts dressing* CLARA *in the rara skirt and cashmere jumper.*

ADA. Time to leave…

CLARA. …and each on our bike with the ten-mile cycle to The New Electric Ballroom spread out ahead like a yellow-brick road.

ADA. The town behind…

CLARA. …and the cobblestone streets sewing it up all neat and perched by the sea, ahh look. We're away, Breda and me, with the… (*Again she's forgotten*.) With the…?

ADA. …with the old road steering…

CLARA (*breaking down*). I can't…

ADA. …with the old road steering us towards The New Electric.

CLARA. Breda, please…

ADA *grabs* CLARA *hard*. ADA *continues the story by herself*.

ADA. And move through the evening with pleated skirts hiding the busy legs beneath. They hide the things that want to be touched by him. They cover all desire and yet smouldering with each yard cycled. The breaths shorter, the freshly pressed blouses a little damp from the sweat. The make-up hot so that the face shimmers. So far behind The Sunshine Ballroom of our poxy harbour town and its lonely fishermen.

BREDA *applies make-up to* CLARA*'s face.*

Them fishermen mauling us like we're the fecking fish. Closing in on us, closing up the dance floor and backed into the corners 'til it's one on one. The lust in their faces. The heavy pants and sweaty palms. Their excuse for dancing? This rhythmless jumping up and down like they've just shit themselves. Which they have. Which they have! How they've trapped our little town in the Stone Age. Perched by the sea, this town needs drowning and reborn. (*Snaps.*) Clara!

CLARA. We cycle on, losing the memory of The Sunshine for The New Electric. The dusty road beneath turning to tarmacadam and the bigger town. The pace kicking us off our bicycles and how we now walk in this new town. Pushing out our little tits with a new confidence now. An American confidence!

ADA. That promise of…

CLARA. 'You meet me after.' His words have me queuing up outside The New Electric and pressed up against its wall.

ADA. Take a breath.

CLARA. For fear I'll blow up, a breath now, Clara.

A pause as CLARA *breathes and gathers herself.*

ADA. Slower.

CLARA (*slower now*). So leaned against the wall. Still have that little girl inside me.

I'm still sat on Mother's knee with hands all flour and cake. I'm still young enough to think of the world as family and town only. I'm at this moment. I'm at the edge of what it is to be a woman. I look from the corner and see all that I'm stepping into, like I'm moving from the black and white to the Technicolor. From nights mauled by fishermen to moments of wanted passion. Behind this wall… his words and desire and my new feelings of…

ADA (*faster now*). And enter then…

CLARA. And enter then…

ADA. And enter then…

CLARA. And enter…

Sounds of a dance floor and music played louder by ADA.

…and all is bodies. Bodies stuck together by numbers and sweat and music and beats and dance and cigarette smoke. And armless, legless bodies held up in a sea of skinny men in dark suits and young women's floral skirts. Already moving in a tide of badly suppressed sex… Oh, we move…

ADA. And Breda…

CLARA. …and Breda…? And Breda then separated, thank Christ. My last tie to home and the life before and Breda's ambition stuck… stuck in the cloakroom and soaked in mineral orange, the sap! Well, not me. Not Clara. Me, passed from stream to stream…

ADA. Louder!

CLARA. Me, passed from stream to stream and nearing the stage with lungs squeezed so tight. A mixture of torture and foreplay I can hear his voice crushing women's hearts and winning the admiration of any man with manhood but not quite the time to open my eyes to my man on stage. (*Slight pause*.) But open then… and there he is! 'The Roller Royle' and his showband. His stance… All-American. His suit a shade of blue right out of summer. His quiff, with no respect to gravity, whipped up on his head and reaching skywards. The Roller Royle. I hear his words from four weeks ago and my heart skips, my breath stops, my head races. 'You meet me after. You meet me after…'

BREDA. Done.

BREDA is finished and CLARA has been fully trans-formed to her eighteen-year-old self.

Well?

ADA (*nods*). Very good.

BREDA sits and looks at the scene as it continues.

CLARA. So afterwards then…

ADA. Wait, Clara!

ADA then turns off the lights so that a single light isolates CLARA in the space.

Afterwards…

CLARA. And backstage and pointed to where the Roller waits. Can hear his hit single, 'Wondrous Place', reel me in, his lovely voice soothing me and making this nervous scene a little easier. The corridor busy with people packing up and moving on to the next town but all thoughts are of him, Ada. Him and the things we will do together. Near his dressing room and my heart slower, my future mapped out with mornings met by his face and his sweet voice singing about this oh-so-wondrous place. The door a little open…

I enter.

A pause. Suddenly CLARA gasps for air and her eyes fill with tears.

He's sat on a table with you stood between his legs. (*Pause.*) He has his face tucked into you. (*Pause.*) His big hands around your tiny waist and he's kissing your mouth.

CLARA *looks to* BREDA.

My throat's jammed with those butterflies. My blood pumped slower. My heart shot all in an instant. It's your blue skirt and red blouse, Breda the bad girl. (*Slight pause.*) I can feel the hooked fingers of Jimbo 'The Face' Byrne tear at my blouse and rip out my heart and claim it as his. I'm stood still… but I'm already running through The New Electric, already travelling the ten miles home and with each yard putting an end to any thoughts of love. Each yard travelled and more distance between me and any wish for what is… (*Almost spits.*) This love. The wind is on my back, and the tide is inching in and the cobblestones uneasy. The winding streets of our harbour town twisting me to the inside. The narrow streets narrower somehow. The houses on either side leaning in too close to me. Telling me, squeezing me, hurrying me towards my inside. Inside where's safe. Get inside, Clara. Get inside. Get inside. Get inside. Get inside…

ADA *turns* CLARA *towards her and stares at her.* ADA *turns the tape recorder off. She then goes and switches the lights back on. She goes to the kitchen cupboard and opens it. Inside, the cupboard is packed with the same type of plain biscuits. She takes out one packet. She hands* CLARA *a biscuit.*

I'm finished for now?

ADA *nods and then gently pats her on the head.*

Will I not have the nice coffee cake I made?

ADA *hands* BREDA *a biscuit.*

Will I not have some tea to wash down this biscuit, Ada?

A long pause. ADA *looks around the space and then at her two sisters eating the plain biscuits. Suddenly, she fires the packet of biscuits against the front door. Biscuits fly everywhere.*

The front door opens. It's PATSY *with another plastic tray full of large fish.*

PATSY. All right, the ladies?

BREDA. Leave them where you stand and go.

PATSY *puts down the tray.* BREDA *goes about cleaning up the biscuits.*

PATSY. Great to see Mary Calley fighting fit after her fall outside Bingo. I heard she had a few to drink and that would account for the terrible thump she gave the ground.

Popped her kneecap right open...

CLARA. That's enough, Patsy.

PATSY. She'll be using the walking stick for another month but that wouldn't put her out much. She only ever does two things as far as I can see, the pub and the Bingo and both of them involve sitting...

BREDA. Patsy!

PATSY. But you'd have to wonder the effects that concentration on a bingo sheet with a stomach full of Malibu has on your average seventy-year-old. That's the thing with age, you see. Medicine is well on top of its treatment to many people but the body of a pensioner is a bit of a lucky bag, isn't it? A routine treatment can uncover all manner of hidden diseases and random ailments. Phyllis Ryan went to the doctor's to get him to move his car and walked away with a burst appendix! I mean, that's a cruel lottery...

BREDA. Leave!

PATSY. Yes, Breda...

BREDA. Now, Patsy, that's enough!

PATSY. Out the door, out the door now, Breda!

PATSY looks towards the open door. Again, he looks very anxious. He can't leave.

Frustrated, he stamps on the ground hard.

SHITE!

The sisters don't react. PATSY then punches himself hard in the stomach. Again the sisters don't react. Again he punches his stomach hard. Again no reaction.

A very long pause.

PATSY. I saw Bernie Doyle in her front garden with all her
    grandchildren having a picnic and I've never seen such an
    amount of jelly in all my life. Mountains of it. (*Slight
    pause*.) I shouldn't have been there, I know that now. I
    shouldn't have. Sometimes my body has a will of its own
    and I find myself walking the little streets with no destina-
    tion in mind. THESE BLOODY LEGS! (*Slight pause*.) I
    was across the road standing on the path and looking at
    the picnic and it was a lovely scene and her son, Bernie's
    son, he's a fisherman and his name is Finbarr, well, he's
    there with his lovely wife and his two kids and I shouldn't
    have done it, ladies, I know I shouldn't have done it, I
    shouldn't have done it!... but I started to imagine me as
    Finbarr. Me on his great big trawler out on the seas...
    though I wouldn't last a day on account of me getting
    seasick all the time... but I'm thinking about what it'd be
    like to have a meal with his lovely wife. What fish we'd
    order. I'm thinking in great detail then. Well, feck it, I stop
    all those thoughts 'cause it's cruel to me and to an outsider
    it's a bit creepy, so I give myself a good kick in the hole
    and I go to my dancing lessons in Sheila and Robert's
    house high on the hill, in their lovely sitting room with
    their paintings on the wall of exotic islands they've never
    visited. The waltzes and tangos and foxtrots and rumbas
    and we're learning the salsa at the moment and that's a
    great laugh, all right! Because there's only the three of us,
    and Sheila and Robert are a couple, I don't get to practise
    with another, so I'm just sitting there in their lovely sitting
    room and watching them dance and I start to think about
    Finbarr and his wife again. 'Stop it, Patsy, that's enough!
    STOP IT NOW!'(*Slight pause*.) And... And then suddenly
    I get this big hole in my stomach. The sort of hole you
    might fall into. And the more I look at Sheila and Robert
    and think of Finbarr and his wife, it feels like the walls of
    this hole are being scooped out by needles so that I'm
    doubled over in the armchair. And Robert's standing over
    me with my mouth all twisting from the pain of these
    needles, you see.... and feck it, I get up fast and leave and
    I'm walking the cobblestones and right above me are the

seagulls gathering and they're sort of laughing at me
'cause I'm holding my stomach and doubled over. And it's
tearing inside and with each second I get glimpses of me
alone. Me in the bed... alone. Me on the streets... alone.
Me staring at the cliffs receding... alone. At the beginning
the seagulls are laughing. My walk quickens with the
fucking seagulls following me and having a laugh. And
then I hear one of them say, 'What is the purpose of you,
Patsy? What is the purpose of you?' Well, I start to run
now, 'cause that's a very hard question to answer and even
harder when it's been asked by a bloody seagull! A seagull
who's got the wings and the where-for-all to get the fuck
out of town and fly off to somewhere else. What is the
purpose of me? Too big a question. Run on, Patsy! And
Mary Calley's looking from the pub with her busted leg
put out on the table. And she sees me running past and her
eyes all big then, her gob already wagging and spreading
the gossip about 'Patsy the mad fishmonger', the bitch!
Well, what 'as she got to gossip about when there's that
amount of Malibu in her she's like her very own
Caribbean island! Run on then! Run on! Run run run run!
(*Pause*.) I stop and I'm standing at your door with these
fish again. Look behind and see the cliffs receding. The
seas being sucked back into the sand. The tides toing and
froing all confused and restless... no sense to them. No
sense to time. I'm back again at your door. (*Slight pause*.)
Well, I start to think and try to get at least one thing clear.
(*Pause*.) The only thing that is certain in my life is that I
always come to this house. I come with the tide, don't I?
And that is a certainty... and that certainty, it soothes me,
somehow. It keeps the bigger question of 'purpose' at bay.
It mightn't stop the seas shrinking or the cliffs receding
but, that certainty, it does... soothe me.

*A pause. The sisters remain quiet. Perhaps they're not even
listening.*

And before now I have never asked for anything. I have
never asked why for all these years you've stayed inside,
Clara and Breda. I don't ask that question for really I have

no business asking. But if coming here is my only certainty and I have the same rhythm as these tides… I wonder now if you ladies would open up to me a little and treat me as a visitor some day. Have a good word to say to me even.

BREDA. Go.

PATSY. I won't return 'less I have a kind word.

BREDA. Don't be stupid, you'll return with the tide.

PATSY. But for what greater purpose?

BREDA. Leave.

PATSY. What purpose, Ada?!

ADA *walks over and holds the door for him.*

Ada?

Slight pause.

ADA. To bring the fish.

PATSY *leaves,* ADA *slamming the door closed behind him.*

CLARA *and* BREDA *go and place each tray of fish in a large chute in the wall as* ADA *stands, lost in her thoughts, looking at the front door.*

ADA *then opens the front door slowly and looks out.*

BREDA, *concerned, looks at* ADA. CLARA *stands looking at the cake.*

CLARA. She never did age, the Virgin Mary. You might put that down to the Middle-Eastern cuisine but Mary Magdalene had a face like a saddle and the truth is, a whore ages worse than someone clean.

BREDA. Clara!

CLARA (*sighs*). Will we ever eat this cake?

BREDA *increasingly concerned over* ADA's *behaviour.*

ADA *remains looking out the front door at the outside as a beautiful golden light slowly fades up outside.*

ADA. I'm sitting in my office floating over the accounts changing fish into numbers.

Seconds and minutes are marking out time but it's the numbers that are marking me out. Making the rhythm of me, balancing me. I look up from the numbers and into the pattern of the day we've made here in this house. When I step out of the office I should be on my way home to your stories and the tea and the cake and Patsy and his fish… But I've stepped on to a beach and my very own new story now. And the sand's like cotton wool underfoot and when I look down the sand's golden. And the air all about me is warm, so it cannot be this island here. And no narrow streets and strange tides and talking seagulls… here the horizon open and light. There's a calm about me because the day has possibilities. And I'm calm because of that.

She covers her eyes with her hand.

But the sea is too still and there's no wind whatsoever and the clouds above are still. Nothing's moving because nothing's real. Like I'm standing in a picture of a beach and not the beach itself. A little child runs past. A six-year-old and I recognise her face when she turns around and smiles. I've seen her in old photographs and I know I'm looking at me running up this beach. She's the girl before you taught me these stories. (*Slight pause.*) I'm looking at her lying face down in a rock pool. I'm pulling her by the hair out of the water.

A pause. She lowers her hand from her eyes.

Things can never change here, can they?

CLARA *and* BREDA *remain silent.*

I really have to leave.

BREDA *walks intently towards the small table where the old tape recorder stands. She starts rewinding the tape. ADA turns and looks at her.*

CLARA (*rubbing her hands together, all excited*). It's time!
    It's time!

ADA. Stop it, Breda!

The tape stops. CLARA *has gone to the door and slams it
shut.*

BREDA *presses the play button and what begins is the
same soundtrack by* ADA *to accompany the stories.*

BREDA. It's time and looking in the mirror and this feeling
    of everything not too right. Up in the bedroom and my sev-
    enteen-year-old body tries to shake off these doubts.
    Staring back behind the blusher and eyeshadow a girl
    who's already been kissed. Been properly kissed. Was it
    only four weeks ago in the car park outside The New
    Electric?

CLARA *starts undressing* BREDA *down to her slip.*

I was stood looking at the ground and every detail of that
spot… the split tarmacadam, a plume of clover, its close
proximity to the chip van… his hand in mine. The details.
The Roller Royle. His hand on my waist and his words.

ADA *confused that it is* BREDA *leading the story.*

ADA. Breda, we don't…

BREDA. The details. The Roller Royle. His hand on my waist
    and his words…

ADA. Stop…

BREDA (*screams*). SAY IT!!

A slight pause.

ADA (*subdued*). 'We'll do it the next…'

BREDA. 'We'll do it the next time, Breda.' Little kiss then.
    Nothing too animal, more of a Gregory Peck. Turns away
    with his chips and my heart and into their van. Four weeks
    then. Four weeks 'til the next time, my first time.

CLARA *takes the 1950's blue pleated skirt and red blouse from the wall.*

ADA (*distant*). Mother calls…

BREDA. And down the stairs on butterflies and into the kitchen and Dad hidden behind the newspaper and the pig face of Clara at her bacon like a dog. The sad hateful face of my sister done up like a clown. How the other girls in the cannery laugh at her behind her stumpy back. Clara, dragging the family down with her mournful eyes and doughy skin. Take to my fry like a bird with my stomach churning with thoughts of the Roller Royle. Perfumed my bra and knickers in anticipation. Stood at the mirror that morning and slid my hands down my pants. Had a chit-chat conversation with myself as him, and took my hands to the rest of me. But tonight's the night. And each on our bike with the ten-mile cycle to The New Electric spread out ahead like a yellow-brick road. The town behind and the cobblestone streets sewing it up all neat and perched by the sea. Well, good enough for drowning and little else! Cycle on and on and feel like one of those Greek heroes taking to the seas, escaping into something better than the poxy Sunshine Ballroom with its oh-so-sad fishermen!

ADA. Buy you a mineral, Breda? Have a biscuit in the car park with me, Breda! (*Chants.*) Breda, Breda, Breda, Breda!

BREDA. And did once with Jimbo 'The Face' Byrne… a man with the biggest face in the west. Handed me his custard cream and asked me to lick the cream from the biscuit. Did so and saw him beating himself off, leaned against his Ford Cortina.

ADA. And enter then…

BREDA. And enter then…

ADA. And enter then…

BREDA. And enter…

Sounds of a dance floor and music played louder by ADA *as* CLARA *adds make-up to* BREDA's *face.*

And all is bodies.

ADA. Louder!

BREDA. And all is bodies…

ADA. Bodies stuck together by numbers and sweat and music and beats and dance and cigarette smoke. And Clara then separated. My last tie to home shunted from my back and Clara's ambition stuck in the Hucklebuck with some sad someone else! But not Breda.

BREDA. Well, not me, lads. Not me. Me already steered towards the backstage. Steered as the Roller Royle serenades his Faithful. The women who'd gladly go all the way and the young men aping the great man himself.

ADA. Backstage…

BREDA. And the showband out front keeping time with my wanting heart. Into the Roller's dressing room and my skin is not my own. All alive it is! Tingling with images and giddy on love! Must settle for fear I blow up… and I do so… I do settle. Settle.

Settle. Settle, Breda. (*Slight pause*.) I start to think of me as a girl. Seventeen and I'm at the edge of things now. Leave behind the safety of all before…

ADA. Leave behind the safety of my home and our little town and step into the real world with love as my only guide.

BREDA *looks at* ADA.

With real love, Breda. Do you understand me?

BREDA *slaps* ADA *hard across the face.* ADA *shaken.*

BREDA *continues.*

BREDA. I can hear the band finishing up with 'Wondrous Place' and for a heartbeat… doubts raise their head. (*Slight pause*.) Door opens and there he is. Words are passed but to no point, no reason. The little room all charged with me and him... so no room for the words as he sits on a table and calls me over. I hold my head back, open my mouth a little and he kisses me softly. His fingers find their way down my back and slide into my pleated skirt and then round front 'til it stops on my belly. Tongues deeper and he lowers his hand then. Lowers it so it's in the perfumed knickers and I push into his hand. And I'm thinking I am his. He is mine certainly. His finger deeper and no doubts now. I can feel him through his pants and I know it's my time. I'm here at the start of a new life and it's my time. Door slams...

CLARA. ...and someone there but gone.

BREDA. 'Stay put, I'll be back, I'll be back, Breda!' (*Quietly.*) Yes.

CLARA *is finished changing* BREDA *into her seventeen-year-old self. She's squeezed into her blouse and skirt.*

CLARA *then hands* BREDA *the show-business suit from the wall.*

CLARA *turns off the lights but for the single light which isolates* BREDA.

BREDA *is suddenly overcome and her eyes fill with tears.* ADA *instinctively takes advantage then.*

ADA (*snaps*). Breda! (*Prompting her.*) Outside then!

BREDA *slowly shakes her head.*

BREDA (*quietly*). I can't.

ADA *goes to her, grabs her by the shoulders and starts shaking her violently.*

ADA. Outside!

ADA *stops.* BREDA *must continue until the end.*

BREDA. Outside and the moon lighting up the scene teasing me more. I can see him walking towards a new face standing in the same spot where I stood. That plume of clover just beneath her in the split tarmacadam. Her...? All Doris Day-like, all sweetness. He's moving in. I can see his big hand on her tiny waist. I can see him mouth the words... 'It's your time...' and little Doris folding into him now. (*Slowly.*) I'm standing, hugging his suit, Ada. My insides start retching. My mouth that he kissed all sour now, where he touched all muck. I'm still but already travelling the ten miles home and with each yard putting an end to any thoughts of love. Each yard travelled and more distance between me and any wish for what it is to be in love. And the wind is on my back and his song mocking me. And the narrow streets of our town they're narrower somehow. The houses on either side leaning in that bit close to me. They're squeezing me, hurrying me towards the inside of this house. To get inside. And stay inside always and keep safe away from this wondrous place. Keep safe. Keep safe inside always.

ADA *turns off the tape and* CLARA *switches back on the lights.*

A long pause. ADA *stares at* BREDA *who stands, alone and beaten.*

ADA. I'm only a baby when I first hear that story from you, Breda. Then thousands of times I've made you tell it again and again like some child... though I am not a child. (*Pause.*) Still, it hurts you just the same, isn't that right?

BREDA. Isn't this what we've tried to teach you? (*Slight pause.*) Don't you feel safer inside than out?

A slight pause.

ADA. I don't feel anything.

ADA *looks towards the front door.*

CLARA *stands looking at the cake again.*

CLARA. What would the Virgin Mary make of all of this, I wonder? Like many women I'd say she keeps an ordered house, but surely she'd have cause to worry for us three. I can almost feel my brain getting softer and it certainly feels like a nearer paradise.

Yes.

A slight pause.

(*Sighs.*) Will we ever eat this cake?

BREDA (*to* ADA). It's time for your rest and then we'll start over.

ADA *nods that she understands. She goes to a room and sits wide awake on the bed.*

BREDA *places the suit back on the wall. A long pause.*

CLARA. There's a lull. Sort of lull that can get you worried. Pass me the bowl, it's time!

BREDA *holds the bowl to her and* CLARA *puts her hand into it. She's very excited. She picks out the one folded up piece of paper that's in there. She unwraps it and reads.*

(*Surprised.*) 'No man is an island'!

BREDA *turns over an hourglass.*

BREDA. Begin.

BREDA *begins to take off her 'costume'.*

CLARA. By their nature people are talkers. You can't deny that. You could but you'd be affirming what you're trying to argue against and what would the point of that be? No point. Just adding to the sea of words that already exist out there in your effort to say that people are not talkers. But people talk and no one in their right mind would challenge that. Unless you're one of those poor souls starved of vocal cords or that Willy Prendergast boy who used live in town and only managed three words. One was 'yes', one was 'no' and one was 'fish'. But even he talked. People are born talkers. Those present when a baby comes into the world are made all too aware that the womb is a more desirable place for a baby. That and the unglamorous entrance the baby must make. For all his miracles and great creations, you'd imagine our Lord could have created a more dignified point of arrival. This is the man who did wonders with the mouth and ears and surpassed Himself with the eyes but sharing a channel with the 'waterworks department' doesn't strike me as the healthiest environment for a yet-to-be-born baby. And I'm not even a plumber. But people get set in their ways early on. Spat out into the world with this feeling of superiority, some people! Stuck in the pram and already the prime spot! Sat opposite me and already the pristine doll...

BREDA. Stuck in the pram, the lumpen pig. Sat opposite me, Mother's little gargoyle...

CLARA. I'm standing looking at your underwear laid out on the bed. I can smell the perfume and it's you who sends me off to the bathroom with a stomach full of doubts!

BREDA. On with the underwear and already you sitting there on my back. Stuck there with your face the picture of this town. The happy pig at the trough with your thoughts of The Sunshine Ballroom. Taking the biscuit in the car park, hey, Clara?! Opening your zip for Jimbo 'The Face'. (*Chants*.) Clara, Clara, Clara, Clara!

CLARA. And cycling the ten miles to The New Electric and you as always po-faced. Like a big plank there! A long streak of misery. Off the bike with tits out and how they look at you, these boys... such indifference.

BREDA. Off the bike and sweat clinging to your hairy back. You smelling like a damp April day though everywhere else is summer. Stood in the queue and again I've got you staining my style. You with your slap-happy face and doughy body stood outside The New Electric like a dressed-up Neanderthal...

CLARA. And enter then...

BREDA. And enter then...

CLARA. And enter then…

BREDA. And enter and get busy throwing you off my back…

CLARA. Throwing you off my back!

BREDA. And 'Wondrous Place' and seconds away from your big heartache.

CLARA. You and the Roller. The big romantic scene…

BREDA. And his hand on my back, and his hand down my front, and his mouth against my mouth. While you're stood there with that face collapsing into tears…

CLARA. And you stood outside in the car park with your sodden perfumed knickers, your stony face for once cracking into some emotion as the Roller rolls on to Doris Day…

BREDA. Bitch!

CLARA. Gobshite!

BREDA. Shut it!

CLARA. A cup of tea a cup of tea a cup of tea!

BREDA. We can't have tea!

CLARA. Where's me tea!?

BREDA. She won't give us any tea.

CLARA. ME CAKE, ME CAKE!!

BREDA (*covering her ears*). We can't have the cake!

CLARA. Me on her lap and I mix the flour with the eggs and the sugar and the coffee…

BREDA. I MADE THE BLOODY CAKE!!

CLARA. And I'm half-listening to the radio and her leg sends me up and down like I'm on a horse trotting.

BREDA *walks fast towards the coffee cake.*

Not galloping now! Never a gallop. She never does anything to harm me, what with me being her favourite! I want
my cake, I want my cake...

BREDA *picks up the coffee cake and violently flings it
towards* CLARA. *It smashes and disintegrates on the floor.*

A pause as they both look down on it.

CLARA *lets out a scream of complete anguish.*

Enter PATSY *fast with more fish.*

PATSY. All right, the ladies?

CLARA (*screams*). GET OUT!

In an act of defiance PATSY *throws the tray of fish on the
ground.*

PATSY. Despite my best efforts to stay away I'm back with
this tide. No rhyme, no reason, no purpose. As always the
bleak welcome...

He goes to leave.

BREDA. Stay.

PATSY *turns back.*

Close the door.

PATSY. You want me to step inside? Like a visitor?

BREDA. Do it.

PATSY *closes the door.*

A long pause. PATSY *can hardly believe he's finally inside.*

CLARA, *sobbing over the cake, mumbles a 'Hail Mary' to
herself.*

Speak to me about your romantic loves.

PATSY. There's nothing to speak of. It's not that I hadn't
wished it but in a town this size we've all got our roles to
play and mine is to play a man of no great purpose...
Might I sit down...

BREDA. Don't be getting ahead of yourself!

PATSY. Yes, Breda.

A slight pause as BREDA *stares at a very self-conscious* PATSY.

BREDA. Off with your clothes.

A slight pause.

PATSY. My clothes?

BREDA. Isn't it like me you are?! Now off with your clothes, Patsy.

PATSY. I don't feel that way about you, Breda....

BREDA. Do it! Clara... Water!

PATSY (*to himself*). Jesus.

PATSY nervously starts taking off his clothes. CLARA *fills a basin of water.*

BREDA. What chance the baby, Patsy? Only born and spat out into dirt. Little baby lying in the cot listening to the words clogging the air. Stepping outside and finding his feet and the poor baby marked by even more words. What chance to keep him clean when the poor creature's turned grubby from the amount of words filling the space, filling your head. Stamped by story, aren't we, Patsy?! So what chance any man or woman against the idle word? The idle word?! Sure, there's no such thing as the idle word. Branded, marked and scarred by talk. Boxed by words, Patsy. Those bitches in the cannery and the gossip rising above the machines. All talk of Clara and Breda and The New Electric and the Roller Royle and the broken hearts. Mocking talk all week turning the streets narrower around us. Them nasty words crashing about from Monday to Friday and locking that front door behind us. What chance for the broken-hearted and the fishmonger to keep clean when people have the making of us? No mystery, no surprise...

CLARA. ...no chance.

BREDA. Marked from early on. What words do you hear branding you, Patsy? 'Lonesome', surely? And 'lumpen' and 'ugly' and 'lonely' and 'foolish' and 'fishy', surely. Surely 'fishy'. Here he is, the 'fishy' fishmonger. And how you might pass and hear all those other words, at once, chasing you, Patsy. Chasing you through the little streets. Well, no more, hey! Isn't it time for a rewrite?

PATSY (*excited*). It's well time, Breda! Well time!

PATSY *stands in his shabby underpants in the basin of water with* CLARA *ready to scrub him clean.*

BREDA. Scrub away then and reborn, Clara!

CLARA *starts vigorously scrubbing him.*

Off with them words and all those stories pasted together and stuck on your back. Wipe away all them lazy images that others pin on us, Patsy. Get clean of that awful smell of fish and guts while you're at it. Strip away letter by letter and them terrible words will surely fall, won't they?! Fall back to the rot where they belong.

CLARA (*struggling with the smell*). Christ!

BREDA. Right out of the hospital and the little baby boy all powdered fresh and standing right here in front us, by Christ! Cleaner than clean with not a single word in earshot against him. No words to name and brand. Like you were spat out of your mother and found yourself standing in your underpants right here in our front room all these years later.

CLARA *continues for a while and then stops scrubbing him.*

CLARA (*catching her breath*). He's done.

PATSY (*smells his skin*). Jesus, like baby skin.

BREDA. And start then.

BREDA *hands the Roller Royle's suit to* CLARA *who starts to dress* PATSY *in it.*

…With the good news spread like wildfire. Standing out into town and the world is claimed as his in an instant. Caught unawares and the world's taken by 'the one and only' as he walks about town and everything moves to his pulse. The cars being pumped along the cobblestones, the little to and fro of people popping in and out of their houses, the shifting patterns of light on the water, even the tides themselves… everything moving for him, from him. The whole world his Faithful. The women who'd gladly go all the way and the young men aping the great man himself.

PATSY. Such pants.

BREDA. Sure, what woman could remain upright with this man about? Some heartless, bloodless, idiot dyke but no other woman, surely? And people's great weapon of words at first seduced and silenced, overawed and struck dumb. At first this silence, but then slowly from a whisper it grows. Oh, it grows, Clara, can't you hear it?

CLARA. Oh, I can, Breda, I can!

BREDA. It starts in a quiet breath and takes to the air, Patsy. A little breeze gets a hold of it and moves it about the house and towards the door and outside. Outside then and a breeze along the cobblestones takes it and through the little sewn-up streets it moves. It moves from breath to breath and the breeze stronger and it stronger too and it's taken to the harbour where the bigger wind takes a hold of it. And passed from breath to breath over the bay and sea and shared out amongst the airstreams it takes to the world and is taken in every breath in every word to everyone. Do you know what it is?

PATSY. Not a clue, Breda.

BREDA. 'Adoration.' Adoration for one man.

CLARA. That suit looks lovely on ya, Patsy.

The new PATSY *transformed in the Roller's suit.*

PATSY (*overawed*). Jesus, Mary and Joseph.

BREDA. Sit down at the table and a new day for us then.

PATSY sits.

ADA walks out from her bedroom and sees PATSY sitting at the table. She stops. He immediately stands.

I thought it time for a visitor.

A pause. PATSY feeling very self-conscious as ADA just stares at him in the suit. She then goes to the table and sits opposite him.

BREDA *puts a plate of two plain biscuits in front of them. He's a little taken aback with the pathetic lunch but PATSY begins to eat it nevertheless. ADA picks up her biscuit and starts to eat it too.*

A very long pause.

PATSY. No chance of a cup of tea? It's a little dry.

There's no answer. He continues to eat the biscuit.

ADA. What is it you have to say to me, Patsy? Something new maybe?

PATSY. Something... new? (*Slight pause.*) Yes.

Deep breath and nervously PATSY stands up and settles himself. He then speaks.

The, emmm... the little cobblestones...

BREDA. Louder, Patsy.

He resumes.

PATSY. The... little cobblestones and they take me to the harbour. I meet you by the harbour, Ada. You're there in your good clothes and me in this terrific suit. And we talk about the fish in the seas and whether the fish have any notion of what awaits them on the land. Christ, if they only knew the torture that awaited them, surely they wouldn't be swimming in packs...

CLARA. New, Patsy! New!

PATSY. So, ahhhh… So, anyway… we're walking through the town and up through the little streets and we can hear the gossip from inside the houses, so you hold my hand then…

BREDA (*prompting him*). And your beautiful face.

PATSY. What?

BREDA. Say it!

PATSY (*fast*). …and then Bernie Doyle, she's there… and we're having a conversation about Nana Cotter's one-hundredth birthday party and the great selection of sand-wiches that were on display…

BREDA. And your beautiful face!

PATSY. And Mr Simmons limps over and we're talking about his new hip.

    Apparently it doesn't need any lubrication which is news to me as I was always under the impression…

BREDA. Patsy!

CLARA (*covers her ears and barks*). Fish yes yes. No yes fish.

PATSY (*panicking*). …We're walking up the hill now, Ada, and the climb of the hill is lesser to us. Past the cannery and into Sheila and Robert's house and Robert's putting on his dancing-instruction video and going through the moves with real precision and dedication, fair play to him…

    ADA *stands and turns away from him.*

    …and I'm no longer sitting in the corner just watching but I'm centre stage with the lovely you now, Ada. Me and the lovely Ada and we're dancing with the pictures of all these exotic islands around us and Robert sipping on a soda water and saying what a great match me and Ada are. 'You're a great match, you two!'… He says…

    ADA *goes towards the front door.*

...And afterwards and we're all having a game of Scrabble which I win with the word 'haddock'... a triple-word winner...

ADA *opens the door and* PATSY *thankfully stops talking.*

A long pause as ADA *looks out on the outside and the three others look at her.*

CLARA. There's a lull. Sort of lull that can get you worried. Pass me the bowl, Breda, it's time!

ADA. You can leave now, Patsy.

PATSY. Romance doesn't come too easy for a fishmonger, Ada. You can see I tried...

ADA. You leave, I stay, that's the order of things here.

PATSY. But maybe a song...

BREDA. Leave, she said.

PATSY. Music can say it better than these awful words, surely!

PATSY *frantically putting a cassette into the tape recorder.*

BREDA. Go, Patsy! Away from the door, Ada!

PATSY. Just one more chance! Fuck it, one more go! Something to fan the flames of love! The music's playing, so the lights to set the scene, Ada, please! Please! Please!

PATSY *stands on the table, ready to sing his song.*

The opening chords to 'Wondrous Place' begins.

The door remains open. ADA *turns off the light inside.* PATSY *lit only by the light streaming through the open door.*

PATSY *sings for* ADA. *He begins nervously.*

> I found a place full of charms,
> A magic world in my baby's arms.
> Her soft embrace like satin and lace –
> Wondrous place.

What a spot in a storm,
To cuddle up and stay nice and warm.
Away from harm in my baby's arms –
Wondrous place.

Man, I'm nowhere
When I'm anywhere else,
But I don't care,
Everything's right when she holds me tight.

Her tender hands on my face,
I'm in heaven in her embrace.
I wanna stay and never go away –
Wondrous place.

Instrumental.

Man, I'm nowhere
When I'm anywhere else,
But I don't care,
Everything's right when she holds me tight.

Her tender hands on my face,
I'm in heaven in her embrace.
I wanna stay and never go away –
Wondrous place.

PATSY *performs wonderfully. It finishes with the air charged with something new.* BREDA *switches the light back on.* PATSY *a little self-conscious.*

A song my poor dead mother taught me.

BREDA (*very hesitant*). Was she pretty, your mother?

PATSY (*staring at* ADA). Like Doris Day, they said. And him a decent singer, though I never learnt of his name or met him even. Last thing I had to do with him was my conception in the car park…

ADA. Of The New Electric Ballroom.

A slight pause.

PATSY. Yeah.

BREDA *remains standing and slowly pisses herself. A small pool forms around her feet.* ADA *looks at this happening and then back to* PATSY.

ADA. Doesn't story always find a way to catch us out, Patsy?

PATSY (*innocently*). It does. Story's a funny fish, all right.

A pause.

ADA (*a little confused*). What a difference you are to me suddenly. (*Pause.*) Time to start anew, you and me?

PATSY. Yes please, Ada.

ADA *stares directly into* PATSY*'s eyes. A pause.*

ADA (*softly*). The town still asleep I cycle to the cannery as always. I sit in my office with the machines crashing inside and tinning the fish. I look over my accounts and turn fish into numbers. I cycle home and the town quiet as always. I see people but talk to no one. A day like any other day. (*Pause. Somewhat nervous.*) But a different day... because of you. Everything coloured by you, every movement, each second passed is touched by you. The town sewn up by you. Tone and air changed knowing that you are close to me. It's me and you, you and me. (*Pause.*) And then it starts as a quiet whisper 'tween two little old ladies who watch us pass by. And it takes to the air. A little breeze gets a hold of it and moves it along the cobblestones and through the sewn-up streets it moves. It moves from breath to breath and the breeze stronger and it stronger too and it's taken to the harbour where the bigger wind takes a hold of it. And passed from breath to breath over the bay and sea and shared out amongst the airstreams it takes to the world and is taken in every breath in every word to everyone. (*Pause.*) The world knows of our new love. It's love.

PATSY. It's love. (*Pause.*) I'm standing in the little shoebox I call my bedroom, Ada.

I'm standing in my underpants and I'm staring down on my little bed. The pillows dented from where we lay our heads. The shape of us marked out on the bed, mapping out

our night's sleep. The house quiet as always. The little
stairs groaning as always. Everything as always but for this
warm feeling in my belly. You're sat in the kitchen waiting
there, Ada. And you touch my face. We're at the edge of
things now and about to leave behind the safety of all
we've known before. So turn to the door and open a life of
possibility…

ADA. And enter then…

PATSY. And enter then…

ADA. And enter then…

PATSY. And enter then…

ADA. And enter then…

PATSY. And enter the outside and the cobblestones and
sewn-up streets and salty air and the possibility for further
away. The outside and destinations unknown and my
world blown right open by 'chance', by this chance to
change. And in an instant I'm part of the living, the free,
the 'fateless', the unmarked and I can see me joining those
seagulls and taking my pick of life, and led by airstream
and breeze, my life made open by your hand in mine. Your
hand is in mine and showing me the open road of possibility, a horizon of chance and what then? Like being
taken to the harbour and just a little drop we are. And
taken by the tides and out further by waves and currents
and further and further still until our little town is a sad
memory, a bad joke.

My life a sudden adventure with my hand in yours. So
what details then? What details, Patsy!? Suddenly I'm
drunk on possibility! We're sheltering from the rain and
you kiss me. I'm curled against your back listening to your
snores. I'm sat on the bed and smiling at you singing in the
bath. I'm holding you in my arms with you twitching
between sleep and wake. I'm watching you laugh at something stupid I said. We're stood in a crowd and you're
touching my back. We're dancing in Sheila and Robert's
with our faces together. We're sitting in Bingo and filling

in the same sheet. We're stood at the harbour and watching the horizon and we take to the sea then and the waves take us and the world opens to us further and further and I'm holding your hand. Your hand holding my hope. Your hand holding my hope. Your hand. (*Pause.*) Christ! Already something's got a hold of me. In one breath all love is good and it keeps me and this love it fills me… but with each step taken and a different love, a fragile love, a love blind, surely. I let go of your hand and walk away fast. And I want for the lover's walk and the lie-ins and the kisses and the sweet remembered details, the slow romance and the sudden lust of love, but my heart tells me that the risk is far too great. It's too great, Ada! We're walking hand in hand but you're not really there. We're sitting side by side but you are somewhere else maybe. I'm curled against your back but your back's colder to me somehow. I'm kissing you with a kiss that lasts seconds too less for me but seconds too more for you. It's not you, it's not you! And what words do you pin to me? 'Lonesome', surely. And 'lumpen' and 'ugly' and 'lonely' and 'fishy', surely. Surely 'fishy'. A man whose only companion is fish and now sewn together with another heart?! Fuck it! My own heart's too scarred by days and nights alone. Too set in its ways by years of chit-chat to little old ladies. Too scared to face into the unknown with just love as a map! I'm stood still but already travelling the lonely road and with each yard travelled it's more distance between me and any wish for what it is to be in love, this reckless love! And the wind is on my back and the seagulls above mocking me! The narrow streets of our town they're narrower. The houses on either side leaning in that bit close. They're squeezing me, hurrying me away from any possibility of a different life! My heart's ripped out and the ground underneath is loose with the cliffs receding. I see the harbour being sucked into the sand and the cliffs pull back like you would pull a curtain back. And now this great space with me running over it towards nothing, towards no home, towards no place, Patsy. My heart ripped out and I can't stop running! I can't stop!

A long pause. ADA, *frozen in shock, is looking towards* PATSY *for some explanation for what she's just heard.* PATSY *can't look at her.* BREDA *and* CLARA *look at* ADA *and await her response. Suddenly* ADA *gasps for air. For the very first time her eyes have filled with tears.* PATSY *turns and leaves fast for the outside. The front door slams shut by itself behind him.*

BREDA *presses the tape recorder and a new story is told.*

BREDA. It's time and looking in the mirror and this feeling of everything not too right.

Stood in the bedroom and your forty-year-old body tries to shake off these doubts.

Staring back a woman who's never been kissed.

CLARA. And it was only yesterday...

BREDA. And it was only yesterday and happy with the pattern of things. When routine woke you with the familiar... the pattern safe, life given a purpose. And what now all of a sudden...?

CLARA *begins to dress* ADA *in the rara skirt and red blouse.*

'Cause still staring back, a woman who's never been kissed. So outside and take to the streets and cycle to the cannery and the machines, to those distant voices and bad words that locked the door. And inside, inside then. And the stories take over and our pattern returns.

CLARA. The lovely pattern of things.

BREDA. By their nature people are talkers. You can't deny that. You could but you'd be affirming what you're trying to argue against and what would the point of that be?

BREDA *aggressively swipes* ADA's *face with lipstick.*

Just adding to the sea of words that already exist out there in your effort to say that people are not talkers. But people talk.

CLARA. Fish fish fish. Yes no fish! No yes fish!

A very long time where BREDA, CLARA *and* ADA *are silent.*

ADA, *costumed ridiculously, face covered in lipstick, stands with tears streaming down her face.* CLARA *sits and stares down on the remains of the sponge cake.*

BREDA *stands still and silent, holding and listening to the tape recorder as the sounds continue for a while. She turns it off.*

Then.

Will we have a cup of tea and some of that nice cake you made, Breda?

BREDA. Yes, Clara.

A pause.

ADA. Will I make the tea, Breda?

BREDA. That would be nice.

ADA *goes to the kettle and turns it on and watches it boil.*

It boils.

Blackout.

Silence.

The End.

Ailís Ní Ríain
TILT

Mark O'Rowe
FROM BOTH HIPS & THE ASPIDISTRA CODE
HOWIE THE ROOKIE
MADE IN CHINA
TERMINUS

Billy Roche
THE CAVALCADERS & AMPHIBIANS
ON SUCH AS WE
THE WEXFORD TRILOGY

Enda Walsh
BEDBOUND & MISTERMAN
DISCO PIGS & SUCKING DUBLIN
THE SMALL THINGS
THE WALWORTH FARCE

Nicholas Wright
CRESSIDA
HIS DARK MATERIALS *after* Pullman
MRS KLEIN
THE REPORTER
THÉRÈSE RAQUIN *after* Zola
VINCENT IN BRIXTON
WRIGHT: FIVE PLAYS

A Nick Hern Book

The New Electric Ballroom first published in Great Britain in 2008 as a paperback original by Nick Hern Books Limited, 14 Larden Road, London W3 7ST, in association with Druid Theatre Company

The New Electric Ballroom copyright © 2008 Enda Walsh

Enda Walsh has asserted his moral right to be identified as the author of this work

The publishers have made every effort to trace all copyright holders, but will be pleased to receive information and make necessary arrangements in the event of any omissions.

Cover image photographed by Ros Kavanagh; designed by John Foley at Bite! Associates, www.bitedesign.com
Cover designed by Ned Hoste, 2H

Typeset by Nick Hern Books, London
Printed and bound in Great Britain by CPI Bookmarque, Croydon, Surrey

A CIP catalogue record for this book is available from the British Library

ISBN 978 1 85459 532 4